Stephen Akintayo, an inspirational Entrepreneur is currently the Chief Executive Officer of Stephen Akintayo Consulting International and Gtext Media and Investment Limited, a leading firm in Nigeria whose services span from digital marketing, website design, bulk sms, online advertising, Media, e-commerce, real estate, Consulting and a host of other services.

Born In Gonge Area of Maiduguri, Borno State. North Eastern part of Nigeria in a very poverish environment and with a civil Servant as a Mother who raise him and his four other siblings with her mega salary since his father's Contract Business had crumbled. Some of his passion for philanthropy was birthed by his humble Beginning.

In his word; "My Surname was poverty. Hunger was my biggest challenge. I had to scavenge all through Primary school to eat lunch as I don't go to school with lunch packs. We were too poor to afford that. Things got better in my secondary school days, though My mum will still go to her colleague to borrow money to send me to school each term.

It was humiliating seeing their disdain faces looking at my mum like a foolish woman who keeps begging. It hurts dearly. I hate Poverty and I pray to help more families come out of it".

Stephen Akintayo story is indeed a grass to grace one. His singular regret in life is that his hard working mother died few year back due to ovarian cancer and never lived to see some of the good works God is using him to do today.

Stephen, Also Founded GileadBalm Group Services which has assisted a number of businesses in Nigeria to move to enviable levels by helping them reach their clients through its enormous nationwide data base of real phone numbers and email addresses. It has hundreds of organizations as its clients including multinational companies like Guarantee Trust Bank, PZ Cussons, MTN,Chivita, among others.

He is also the Founder and President of Infinity Foundation and Stephen Akintayo Foundation, an indigenous non-governmental organization that assists orphans and vulnerable children as well as mentor young minds.

The foundation has assisted over 2,000 orphans and vulnerable children and has also partnered with 22 orphanage homes in the country. By December 2015 Infinity Foundation is starting Mercy Orphanage to care for victims of Boko haram attacks in the Northern part of Nigeria.

Stephen Akintayo Foundation focus on Financial Grants with Initial grant of 10,000,000 to 20 entrepreneur in 2015 plan to grow that to 500Million annual grant by the 5th year. Projects like Upgrade Conference and The Serial Entrepreneur Conference with thousands of attendee who benefit from the high value knowledge from exceptional speakers and consultants.

Stephen, popularly called Pastor Stephen is also the founder of Omonaija, an online radio station in Lagos currently streaming for 24 hours daily with the capacity to reach every country of the world.

He is the founder and Director of Digital Marketing School Nigeria. Africa's leading Digital Marketing school issuing diploma certificates with robust training curriculum in Digital Maketing,Tele Marketing and Neuro Marketing.

He is an Author of several published books including Turning Your Mess To Message, Soul Mate, Survival Instincts and Mobile Millionaire Stephen is a media personality in the Television, Radio and Print media.
He is currently anchoring a programme on Radio Continental, tagged CEO Mentorship with Stephen Akintayo, and A TV Show coming airing in the last quarter of 2015 as well as currently running a weekly column in some of Nigeria's national papers, including The Nation Newspaper and The Union
Newspapers. He is also a social media guru.

His mentorship platform has helped thousands of people including graduates and undergraduates in the area of business as well as in relationships.

Stephen strongly believes young Nigerians with the passion for entrepreneurship can cause a business revolution in Nigeria and the world at large.

Stephen Akintayo is currently running Masters In Digital Marketing and MBA in Netherlands.

He is a trained Digital Marketing Consultant by the Digital Marketing Institute and Harvard University. He is also a trained Coach by The Coaching Academy UK. He has several other professional training inside and outside Nigeria.

He is First Degree is in Microbiology from Olabisi Onabanjo University, a member of Institute of Strategic Management. He is an ordained Pastor with Living Faith Church Worldwide and he is happily married and blessed with Two Sons; Divine Surprises and Future.

To invite Stephen Akintayo for a speaking engagement kindly email: invite@stephenakintayo.com or call:08188220066.

Copyright 2013

<u>IMPORTANT LEGAL STUFF</u>

This book is © Mr. Stephen Akintayo All Rights Reserved. You may not sell this book, give it away, display it publicly, nor may you distribute it in any form whatsoever.

While reasonable attempts have been made to ensure the accuracy of the information provided in this publication, the author does not assume any responsibility for errors, omissions or contrary interpretation of this information and any damages or costs incurred by that.

This book is not intended for use as a source of legal, business, accounting or financial advice. All readers are advised to seek the services of competent professionals in legal, business, accounting and finance fields.

While examples of past results may be used occasionally in this work, they are intended to be for purposes of example only. No representation is made or implied that the reader will do as well from using any of the techniques mentioned in this book.

The contents of this book are based solely on the personal experiences of the author. The author does not assume any responsibility or liability whatsoever for what you choose to do with this information. Use your own judgment.

Any perceived slight of specific people or organizations, and any resemblance to characters living, dead or otherwise, real or fictitious, is purely unintentional. You are encouraged to print this book for easy reading. However, you use this information at your own risk.

TABLE OF CONTENT

1. About the Author ………………………..Pg. 2
2. Important legal stuff ………………….Pg. 4
3. Table of content…………………………..Pg. 3
4. What is Email Marketing? ……………Pg. 6
5. Types of Email Marketing …………….Pg. 8
6. Why Email Marketing? ………………..Pg. 13
7. Benefits of Email Marketing for businesses..Pg. 16
8. Steps to set up an email marketing platform...Pg. 19
9. Creating an Email Campaign………….Pg. 24
10. Tips to creating a high converting email campaign…..Pg. 32
11. Final Words on Email Marketing…...Pg.35

CHAPTER ONE
WHAT IS EMAIL MARKETING?

WHAT IS EMAIL MARKETING?

Email marketing is a direct marketing platform by which a commercial message is sent to a group of people using **email** (electronic mail).

In deeper marketing terms, every email sent to a potential or current customer is a form of email marketing.

In email marketing, emails can be used to send ads, request business patronage, or solicit sales or donations, with the sole aim of building loyalty, trust, or brand awareness.

Email marketing can be done to either opt in lists or a current customer database.

Majorly, the term 'email marketing' is usually used to refer to sending email messages with an aim of enhancing the relationship of a business (product or service provider) with its current or previous customers, to establish **customer loyalty** for continuous patronage, acquiring new customers or convincing current customers to purchase something immediately.

CHAPTER TWO
TYPES OF EMAIL MARKETING

EMAIL MARKETING CAN BE CARRIED OUT THROUGH DIFFERENT TYPES OF EMAILS:

Transactional emails

Transactional emails are usually triggered based on a customer's action with a company.

To be qualified as transactional or relationship messages, these communications' primary purpose must be "to facilitate, complete, or confirm a commercial transaction that the recipient has previously agreed to enter into with the sender", along with a few other narrow definitions of transactional messaging.

Triggered transactional messages include dropped basket messages, password reset emails, purchase or order confirmation emails, order status emails, reorder emails and email receipts.

The primary purpose of a transactional email is to convey information regarding the action that triggered it. But, due to its high open rates (51.3% compared to 36.6% for email newsletters), transactional emails are an opportunity to engage customers: to introduce or extend the email relationship with customers or subscribers, to anticipate and answer questions or to cross-sell or up-sell products or services.

Many email newsletter software vendors offer transactional email support, which gives companies the ability to include promotional messages within the body of transactional emails. There are also software vendors that offer specialized transactional email marketing services, which include providing targeted and personalized transactional email messages and running specific marketing campaigns (such as customer referral programs).

Direct emails

Direct email or interruption based marketing involves sending an email solely to communicate a promotional message (for example, an announcement of a special offer or a catalog of products). Companies usually collect a list of customer or prospect email addresses to send direct promotional messages to, or they can also rent a list of email addresses from service companies, but safe mail marketing is also used.

Comparison to traditional mail

There are both advantages and disadvantages to using email marketing in comparison to traditional advertising mail.

Advantages

Email marketing is popular with companies for several reasons:

- An exact return on investment can be tracked ("track to basket") and has proven to be high when done properly. Email marketing is often reported as second only to search marketing as the most effective online marketing tactic.
- Email marketing is significantly cheaper and faster than traditional mail, mainly because of high cost and time required in a traditional mail campaign for producing the artwork, printing, addressing and mailing.
- Advertisers can reach substantial numbers of email subscribers who have opted in (i.e., consented) to receive email communications on subjects of interest to them.

Almost half of American Internet users check or send email on a typical day, with email blasts that are delivered between 1 am and 5 am local time outperforming those sent at other times in open and click rates.

- Email is popular with digital marketers, rising an estimated 15% in 2009 to £292 m in the UK.
- If compared to standard email, direct email marketing produces higher response rate and higher average order value for e-commerce businesses.

Disadvantages

A report issued by the email services company Return Path, as of mid-2008 email deliverability is still an issue for legitimate marketers. According to the report, legitimate email servers averaged a delivery rate of 56%; twenty percent of the messages were rejected, and eight percent were filtered. Companies considering the use of an email marketing program must make sure that their program does not violate spam laws such as the United States' Controlling the Assault of Non-Solicited Pornography and Marketing

Act (CAN-SPAM). The European Privacy and Electronic Communications Regulations 2003, or their Internet service provider's acceptable use policy.

Opt-in email advertising

Opt-in email advertising, or permission marketing, is a method of advertising via email whereby the recipient of the advertisement has consented to receive it. This method is one of several developed by marketers to eliminate the disadvantages of email marketing.

Opt-in email marketing may evolve into a technology that uses a handshake protocol between the sender and receiver. This system is intended to eventually result in a high degree of satisfaction between consumers and marketers.

If opt-in email advertising is used, the material that is emailed to consumers will be "anticipated." It is assumed that the consumer wants to receive it, which makes it unlike unsolicited advertisements sent to the consumer. Ideally, opt-in email advertisements will be more personal and relevant to the consumer than untargeted advertisements.

A common example of permission marketing is a newsletter sent to an advertising firm's customers. Such newsletters inform customers of upcoming events or promotions, or new products. In this type of advertising, a company that wants to send a newsletter to their customers may ask them at the point of purchase if they would like to receive the newsletter.

With a foundation of opted-in contact information stored in their database, marketers can send out promotional materials automatically using autoresponders—known as Drip Marketing. They can also segment their promotions to specific market segments.

Legal requirements

Australia

The Australian Spam Act 2003 is enforced by the Australian Communications and Media Authority, widely known as "ACMA". The Act defines the terms unsolicited electronic messages, how unsubscribe functions must work for commercial messages and other key information. Fines range with 3 fines of $110,000 AUD being issued to Virgin Blue

Airlines (2011) Tiger Airways Holdings Limited (2012) and Cellarmaster Wines Pty Limited (2013).

Canada

The "Canada Anti-Spam Law" (CASL) went into effect on July 1, 2014. CASL requires an explicit or implicit opt-in from users, and the maximum fines for noncompliance are CA$1 million for individuals and $10 million for businesses.

European Union

In 2002 the European Union (EU) introduced the Directive on Privacy and Electronic Communications. Article 13 of the Directive prohibits the use of personal email addresses for marketing purposes. The Directive establishes the opt-in regime, where unsolicited emails may be sent only with prior agreement of the recipient, this does not apply to business email addresses.

The directive has since been incorporated into the laws of member states. In the UK it is covered under the Privacy and Electronic Communications (EC Directive) Regulations 2003 and applies to all organizations that send out marketing by some form of electronic communication.

United States

The CAN-SPAM Act of 2003 was passed by Congress as a direct response of the growing number of complaints over spam e-mails. Congress determined that the US government was showing an increased interest in the regulation of commercial electronic mail nationally, that those who send commercial e-mails should not mislead recipients over the source or content of them, and that all recipients of such emails have a right to decline them.

The act authorizes a US $16,000 penalty per violation for spamming each individual recipient. However, it does not ban spam emailing outright, but imposes laws on using deceptive marketing methods through headings which are "materially false or misleading". In addition there are conditions which email marketers must meet in terms of their format, their content and labeling. As a result, many commercial email marketers within the United States utilize a service or special software to ensure compliance with the Act.

A variety of older systems exist that do not ensure compliance with the Act. To comply with the Act's regulation of commercial email, services also typically require users to authenticate their return address and include a valid physical address, provide a one-click unsubscribe feature, and prohibit importing lists of purchased addresses that may not have given valid permission.

In addition to satisfying legal requirements, email service providers (ESPs) began to help customers establish and manage their own email marketing campaigns. The service providers supply email templates and general best practices, as well as methods for handling subscriptions and cancellations automatically. Some ESPs will provide insight/assistance with deliverability issues for major email providers. They also provide statistics pertaining to the number of messages received and opened, and whether the recipients clicked on any links within the messages.

The CAN-SPAM Act was updated with some new regulations including a no fee provision for opting out, further definition of "sender", post office or private mail boxes count as a "valid physical postal address" and definition of "person". These new provisions went into effect on July 7, 2008.

CHAPTER THREE
WHY EMAIL MARKETING?

WHY EMAIL MARKETING?

Five Great Reasons.

Email marketing is one of the most powerful marketing tools available to businesses of all types and sizes. Here are five great reasons to give email marketing a try.

Why Email Marketing?

Experts and small businesses agree:

"54% OF SMALL BUSINESSES SURVEYED RATED E-MAIL AS THE TOP ONLINE PROMOTION TO DRIVE SITE VISITORS AND CUSTOMERS TO THEIR WEB SITES AND STOREFRONTS." DMA INTERACTIVE

10   It's   Inexpensive.
Email marketing is an affordable way to stretch a tight marketing budget - and whose isn't these days? Opposite to direct mail, there is virtually no production, materials or postage expense. In addition, there are self-service solutions available that let you remove agency creative costs as well. Email marketing is 20 times more cost effective than direct mail, and can cost as little as fractions of a penny per email.

2)   It's   Effective
Email marketing enables you to proactively

communicate with your existing customers and prospects instead of slowly waiting for them to return to your Web site or storefront. You can easily target your emails by source, interest, or list.

Overall, email communications sent to your prospect and customer lists, can single-handedly improve the ROI (Return on Investment) of all of your lead generation and customer retention programs.

3) It's Immediate

Email marketing has two great advantages over other marketing platforms. First, with the self-service tools available, anyone can create and send compelling email newsletters, promotions, announcements or more in hours or days. No agency or production time is required to create and send professional email campaigns. Second, email marketing generates an immediate response. The call to action is clear: "Click here to take advantage of this offer", or "to learn more about this service", or to "attend this event". Initial campaign response generally occurs within 48 hours of the time the email campaign is sent.

4) It's Measurable

As an advantage over other marketing platforms, results from email campaigns are easily measured. Results are reported in terms of "opens", which report how many people saw your offer or newsletters. Click through Rates (CTRs), which measure how many people actually clicked on the links in your email, and in a many cases, who actually clicked on those links.

5) It's Easy

There are Web-based email marketing products for small and medium businesses. Most include professional HTML templates, list segmentation and targeting functionalities, as well as, automatic tracking and reporting. So, you are free to focus on your unique message while the rest is done for you.

It is time to put email marketing to work for your business! Let's get started!

CHAPTER FOUR
BENEFITS OF EMAIL MARKETING FOR BUSINESSES.

5 Reasons You Should Start An Email Marketing Campaign:

1. Email Marketing is Targeted
EMAIL MARKETING SOLVES ALL THE ANCIENT PROBLEMS OF NON-TARGETED MARKETING. GONE ARE THE DAYS OF PLACING AN ADVERTISEMENT ON TELEVISION, ON A DINER PLACEMAT, OR IN A MAGAZINE WITH NO CONTROL OF WHO WILL SEE IT. WITH EMAIL MARKETING, YOU HAVE THE ABILITY TO CONTROL EXACTLY WHO SEES YOUR EMAIL BY SEGMENTING YOUR CONTACTS BASED ON THEIR LEAD STATUS, DEMOGRAPHICS (CHARACTERISTICS), LOCATION OR ANY OTHER DATA. TARGETING EMAILS ENSURES THAT YOUR AUDIENCE RECEIVES INFORMATION TAILORED SPECIFICALLY TO MEET HIS/HER NEEDS. EMAIL MARKETING MAKES IT SIMPLE TO CUSTOMIZE YOUR MESSAGE FOR EACH CUSTOMER, THEREBY BRINGING A HIGHER CONVERSION OR SALES RATE.

2. Email Marketing Increases Brand Awareness
WITH EACH EMAIL SENT, CONSUMERS ARE EXPOSED TO YOUR BUSINESS AND YOUR BRAND. WITH STRATEGIC PLANNING, SMART DESIGN AND TARGETED

INFORMATION, YOUR BUSINESS WILL CONSISTENTLY BUILD VALUE. IN DOING SO, YOU STAY ON TOP-OF-THE-GAME WITH YOUR AUDIENCE. THEN, WHEN A CUSTOMER NEEDS PRODUCTS OR SERVICES, YOUR BUSINESS STANDS A MUCH BETTER CHANCE OF TURNING THOSE LEADS INTO CLIENTS AND CLIENTS INTO LOYAL CUSTOMERS.

3. Email Marketing is Easily Shareable. THERE AREN'T MANY FORMS OF MARKETING AS EASY TO SHARE AS EMAIL MARKETING. WITH THE SIMPLE CLICK OF THE FORWARD BUTTON, SUBSCRIBERS CAN SHARE YOUR DEALS, OFFERS AND NEWS WITH THEIR FRIENDS. SUBSCRIBERS WHO SHARE YOUR EMAILS ARE ACTING AS BRAND ADVOCATES. THEREFORE, WHEN A SUBSCRIBER SHARES AN EMAIL WITH FRIENDS, YOUR BRAND GAINS MORE EXPOSURE AND CREDIBILITY AND VALUE.

4. Email Marketing is Measurable ANALYTICS ARE A MUST TO MEASURING THE SUCCESS OF ANY CAMPAIGN. MANY MARKETING CHANNELS PRESENT UNCLEAR AND ESTIMATED RESULTS. EMAIL MARKETING, ON THE OTHER HAND, DRAWS PRECISE, ACCURATE AND VALUABLE STATISTICS, INCLUDING DELIVERY RATES, OPEN RATES, CLICK-TO-DELIVER RATES AND SUBSCRIBER RETENTION RATES. EVEN BETTER: THESE STATISTICS ARE MORE THAN JUST NUMBERS AND PERCENTAGES. THEY ARE INSIGHTS ABOUT YOUR CUSTOMER'S BEHAVIORS AND INTERESTS. USE YOUR EMAIL MARKETING CAMPAIGN AS A TOOL TO MONITOR WHICH INFORMATION YOUR CONSUMERS LIKE AND RESPOND TO THE MOST. FROM THERE, YOU CAN FURTHER TARGET YOUR MARKETING STRATEGY TOWARDS MORE SUCCESSFUL CAMPAIGNS AND TOPICS OF INTEREST.

5. Email Marketing is Cost effective. PERHAPS THE MOST APPEALING ADVANTAGE OF EMAIL MARKETING IS THE RETURN ON INVESTMENT. NO PRINT COSTS, NO POSTAGE FEES, NO ADVERTISING RATES. EMAIL MARKETING IS A SUPER AFFORDABLE MARKETING PLATFORM. ACCORDING TO THE DIRECT MARKETING ASSOCIATION, EMAIL MARKETING BRINGS IN $40 FOR EVERY $1 SPEND, OUTPERFORMING SEARCH, DISPLAY AND SOCIAL MARKETING.

Email Marketing is a must.

In today's ever-changing digital world, email marketing tends to take a backseat. However, if you haven't considered email marketing for your business already, now is the time to do so. Email marketing is a targeted, shareable, credible, measurable, and cost-effective tool which is overlooked by many. Working with a trusted marketing advisor makes the process simple and cost-effective. With a strategic approach, proper guidance and a strong message, your business is sure to benefit, and make huge gains from email marketing.

Now, after all this insightful information on the benefits of email marketing for your business, I can imagine you're so interested in knowing how to set up this platform for your business.

Now, let's get into: "Steps to set up an email marketing platform".

CHAPTER FIVE
STEPS TO SET UP AN EMAIL MARKETING PLATFORM

STEPS TO SET UP AN EMAIL MARKETING PLATFORM

Before we move into the technical part of setting up an email marketing platform, we must first settle our LISTS. If our email marketing will ever be successful, it must be sent to people through their email addresses, and we must have a way of getting those emails addresses. This brings us to the first section of setting up an email marketing platform: 'How to build an effective mailing list?'

How to build an effective mailing list?

1. Build Your List the Slow & Steady Way

When I was first starting out online, the slow and steady way is how I built my list. It's the default way to build up an audience, and it's not bad but it does take time. This is a perfect strategy to help you build your traffic and list over time, because it's consistent: you create content, blog, guest post, apply SEO techniques, get word of mouth, and repeat on a regular basis.

This is effective if you've got an actual business to run, or maybe you have a day job and this is your side project. It's simple enough to dedicate a few hours per week to showing up and creating content. Over time your site's authority will increase in the search engines, you'll develop word of mouth from your fans, and things will slowly pick up the pace.

The problem? It's slow, so if you want to results fast, it's not going to happen for you.

Many bigger sites started out with the slow and steady path, like Digital Marketing School, and my first business Gilead Balm SMS. These sites weren't overnight successes, but now they get steady traffic from the search engines and when people think of the topics for these sites they can point people to them, generating word of mouth.

2. Use Short Focused Campaigns to Build Your List

For this strategy, you set aside a month or two dedicated to traffic and list building. During these few months, you put everything you've got into building your list. Because it's timed, it has more of an immediacy factor, and it feels more urgent and fresh.

The types of tactics you'd use for a short focused campaign are putting on a live webinar or live stream, running a contest, doing a joint venture, or running ads to your opt-in squeeze page (since you might not want to run ads 365 days a year but you might do it for a short period of time). A squeeze page is a pop up type of form in which you offer your campaign, but requires the visitor on your site to input his/her email address to access the offers. This serves as a funnel for effective and quick list building.

All of these things have an end point, so you can set aside time in your yearly calendar to focus on traffic and list building. If you run a seasonal business, this might be the type of activity you do during your off season.

Here's an example from Amy Porterfield running a joint webinar withMelanie Duncan about Pinterest. This works great because it's a specific point in time, and the nature of joint webinars is both parties build their lists.

Another example is the 30 Day List Building Challenge, which is a contest that runs for a short period of time. It's also got social sharing built into it, which is also something that works best in short focused bursts.

---

3. Make a Big Splash with a Launch

You've definitely seen the big splash model, it's usually attached to a product launch and it seems to take over a corner of the internet for a while. You know someone is doing a launch when suddenly you see their name everywhere at once, they're being interviewed, guest posting, and showing up every now and then on social media.

The big splash works wonders because you capture the attention of the entire market. It's being at everywhere at once advantage. But to understand how to pull off a launch, you need to know exactly how much time goes into it. The reason a big splash is different from a short burst is because there are usually months of time dedicated to the launch leading up to it. And by months, I mean upwards of 4 months for really big launches.

Securing all the guest spots, interviews, affiliates, and making sure all the buzz goes live at the same time is no easy task. But when a launch comes together, it really has the potential to drive so much traffic and grow your list like nothing else.

You've no doubt seen big launches, but among a few to remember is the launch of Etisalat Nigeria. Their launch campaign announced them out and almost immediately after their launch, millions of Nigerians had subscribed on their network. The same works for building your list as well. There are entire courses on how to pull together a killer launch, and if you're offering a new product or service you'll want to spend some time figuring out your positioning and creating the best product you can, as a launch can bring you huge traffic and create a great list for you.

4. Focus on Reaching New Niches.

One often ignored strategy for list building is to step outside of your present market, and get known in a new niche. Take for example, my list building advice: it works for bloggers, but it can also work for photographers, dentists, and jewelry designers. I've been able to repurpose my content and do short focused bursts of list building in these different markets.

You can actually choose any of the previous 3 strategies to go into new niches, you could do a big launch in a new niche or go the slow and steady route. **The benefit here is you can usually**

jumpstart your efforts because of the previous work you've done in your main market, and you can get more specific in how you serve people.

Someone who has done a great job of becoming known in many niches is Aliko Dangote. He sits at the intersection of many markets like oil & gas, entrepreneurship, building construction, flour & milling and so on. I personally stumbled upon this idea with my different blogs and businesses in marketing (online & offline) and real estate, when I realized there was a lot of overlap and people would follow me from one business to the next.

Can you think of a few "sub markets" you could focus on, in order to help you reach new people and grow your list further?

Now that we've learnt how to create or build our list, let move to how we can create an email campaign & the platforms online or offline we can use to do so.

CHAPTER SIX
CREATING AN EMAIL CAMPAIGN

CREATING AN EMAIL CAMPAIGN

In creating an email campaign there are two major platforms which can be used.
1. Online Email Marketing Service Providers.
2. Dedicated Email Marketing Server Software.

Online Email Marketing Service Providers

Online email marketing service providers are companies online with online servers that can send emails in bulk to any generated list.

There are many online email marketing services available to choose from, and they vary based on their email sending limits per month, and their pricing plans. The average email sending limits per month varies from 1,000 to 2,000 emails per day on one account.

Each of these online email service providers require you to create an account on their website, from which you can manage your mailing lists and send email marketing campaigns.

Below are the list of some of the many online email marketing service providers.

1. Mail Chimp – MailChimp is one of the most-frequently used email applications, with customized signup forms you can integrate into your website or your Facebook page, social sharing integration, dozens of customizable templates and a full-featured API to sync existing customer databases, shopping carts and more. MailChimp is ideal for beginners, since it's free for up to 2,000 subscribers — and you can send up to 12,000 emails per month. However, you are limited on a few features under the free plan. Paid plans are full-featured and very affordable, ranging from $10 to $240 per month, depending on the number of subscribers—all with the ability to send unlimited emails.

2. Constant Contact – If you've heard of email marketing, you've probably heard of Constant Contact. It's one of the most comprehensive email marketing

applications on the web, with a variety of ancillary tools, such as surveys and event marketing, that you can add-on with a fee. Constant Contact's built-in analytics are pretty awesome, as well as its impressive customizable template database and social sharing features. You can get started with Constant Contact for as little as $15 per month, after a 60-day free trial.

3. AWeber – Aweber features auto responder follow-up, customizable HTML email marketing templates, signup forms, RSS-to-email (create emails automatically from your latest blog posts), a full-featured API and much more. Not to mention a robust learning database featuring live webinars, video training, a complete knowledge base to help you navigate the features and a blog with insider tips on maximizing your email marketing campaigns. Pricing starts at just $19 per month for up to 500 subscribers.

4. iContact – iContact has also made a name for itself in the email marketing scene, offering hundreds of email marketing templates to choose from, an easy drag-and-drop interface for users without advanced design skills, and integrated social sharing features so you can share your messages with Facebook, Twitter and LinkedIn. Deep contact history offers an in-depth view of your previous interactions with each subscriber, so you can manage your relationships more effectively. Pricing ranges from $14 for 500 subscribers to $47 for 5,000 subscribers per month.

5. Vertical Response – Vertical Response offers email marketing as one component of its host of marketing products, which also includes social media marketing, event marketing, online surveys and other applications. With more than 700 email templates to choose from, real-time analytics and easy sharing functions, Vertical Response is a comprehensive

email platform. Vertical Response offers a pay-as-you-go, per-email price structure—so you're only paying for the services you actually use.

6. Campaign Monitor – **Create your own templates with Campaign Monitor's easy-to-use template builder. Choose from a variety of layouts, choose colors and then customize your text, images and even personalized messaging. Campaign Monitor's emails are automatically optimized for mobile too—the perfect solution for today's mobile-driven users. Signup is free, and you can send campaigns starting at just $9 per month.**

7. Pure 360 – **Pure 360 offers an impressive set of products and features for email marketers. Behavioral re-targeting, Facebook register to encourage signups and send targeted emails as a result, RSS-to-email, and split content and subject line testing are just some of the capabilities this powerful platform offers. Because**

this is a comprehensive platform with robust capabilities, it's a bit pricier than some of the others listed here, and designed for users who send more than 50,000 emails per month. You can request a price quote using this form.

8. The Mission Suite – The Mission Suite looks at email marketing as a social network that's been around much longer than Facebook and Twitter. With prices ranging between $15 and $300 per month, The Mission Suite packs a slew of handy features into an affordable email marketing platform. Take advantage of built-in solutions, such as event marketing, viral coupon campaigns, surveys, social media integration and even opt-in text messaging.

9. Campaigner – Campaigner offers a 30-day free trial, so you can test out this platform's functionality before you commit to a monthly budget. Use functions such as recurring and triggered

campaigns, advanced list management with segmentation and more to maximize your results.

10. Emma – Emma offers ready-made email templates, cool visuals including response graphs and analytics data, unlimited free surveys, Google Analytics integration and more. Emma's analytics helps you look beyond the surface data to identify trends over time and dig deep into data for maximum results. Pricing starts at $30 per month for up to 1,000 subscribers and goes up to $420 per month for 75,000 subscribers. If you have a super-fabulous list of more than 75,000 peeps, Emma will create a custom plan to meet your needs.

11. dotMailer – dotMailer is an easy-to-use, super-fast platform that's scalable for your email, social, mobile, design, management and reporting needs. Pricing structures are offered for small-to-medium businesses as well as large enterprises. You can start out with a

simple, free account with 500 free sends, then move to a pay-as-you-go plan starting at $9.99 per month.

12. Jango Mail – **Jango Mail** is a totally customizable email platform with 100% branding control (no "Powered By" branding in the footer of your emails), simple HTML editors, and comprehensive preview tools so you can see exactly what your subscribers will see before you send, self-configured auto-response and much more. Price plans start at just $15 for 1,000 emails sent per month, and agency plans are also available.

13. Benchmark Email – **Benchmark Email's** editor works just like a Word document, for totally streamlined and simplified design—even if you're not a skilled designer. You can customize signup forms for Facebook, Twitter, or your website, and track important metrics like open rates and social shares. Benchmark

Email starts at $9.95 per month for up to 600 sent emails.

14. GetResponse – GetResponse lets you "create stunning newsletters and landing pages in minutes," with capabilities including 1-to-1 personalized messaging, customized offers, and more with targeted accuracy and perfect timing. GetResponse's drag-and-drop editor makes it simple for anyone—designer or total non-designer—to create captivating email messages with ease. GetResponse starts at just $15 per month for up to 1,000 subscribers. If you make an annual purchase, you get a sweet discount, too.

15. StreamSend – As its name suggests, StreamSend streamlines email marketing with easy opt-in/opt-out features, opt-in confirmations, list management including importing and exporting of contacts, list segmentation and more. And that's just on the administrative end. You can also take advantage of Email Analyzer, which

tests your messages in 30 different email clients. If you've ever sent an email marketing campaign, you're probably painfully familiar with the hassle of different email clients rendering your code in various, and sometimes absurdly wacky, ways. Plans start at $19.90 per month for up to 2,000 emails.

16. Graphic Mail – With GraphicMail, you'll not only know who opened your email, but what device they used, what links they clicked and whether they shared it across their social networks. Choose from more than 300 customizable email templates and make them your own with a simple, intuitive design interface. Choose from multiple pricing options, based either on the number of contacts you have (limited to one email per day) or the volume of emails you send.

17. Email Brain – Email Brain offers comprehensive analytics to help you monitor and improve your campaigns,

including viral tracking report analysis, campaign bounce reports, open and click rates and much more. An integrated, WYSIWYG editor lets you easily customize and create powerful and visually appealing email messages and newsletters. Pricing starts at $9.95 per month for up to 2,000 emails.

18. Mailigen – Social media integration, mobile marketing, integration with popular tools and applications, real-time reporting and analysis and a drag-and-drop editor are just some of the features you'll get with Mailigen. Prices start as low as $10 per month or 4 cents per email.

19. MailerLite – For just $99 per year (for up to 10,000 subscribers), you can take advantage of MailerLite's many features, such as mobile-friendly emails, drag-and-drop editor, real-time reporting, comprehensive list management and more.

20. SendLoop – SendLoop is "the easy way to send email newsletters." List management, campaign management, integration with awesome apps such as EventBrite, HighRise and WordPress, and even a full-featured API for developers are included in the $35-per-month fee for up to 2,500 subscribers.

21. Elite Email – Choose from more than 400 ready-to-use templates, share your emails on popular social platforms such as Facebook, Twitter, LinkedIn and Google+, take advantage of a fully-branded subscription center where your customers can set up their preferences, enter their info and even edit their profiles (talk about making you look sophisticated!), and fall in love with the live ticker that delivers your stats as they're happening. (Ideal for those of us who are less-than-patient when we're waiting for metrics!). It's FREE for up to 500 email address. Yes, free. More than 500 contacts? Prices start at $15 per

month. Totally affordable, and totally awesome.

22. Interspire Email Marketer – **Interspire is a cool platform with features to help you automate your list management, optimize your click-through rates, solicit and track feedback with surveys, and advanced reporting allowing you to see the full activity of a single lead for maximum personalization and analysis. Pricing starts at $495 for a single user—yes, it seems a little pricey on the surface, but this is a lifetime license for a slew of capabilities. In other words, definitely worth it!**

23. Simply Cast – **SimplyCast is an email marketing platform offering custom templates (for a one-time $99 fee), email client rendering so you're sure your campaigns won't look like gobbled-gook to your subscribers, and even subaccounts so you can give other users access with specific permissions. A campaign cross-**

check ensures you're not missing any important details before your message goes out. It's free for up to 2,000 email contacts. Doesn't get any better than that! Paid plans are incredibly affordable as well, if you have a larger list.

24. SendGrid – SendGrid provides reliability, scalability, comprehensive, real-time analytics and more—including a full-featured API. Prices start at $9.95 per month for an incredible 40,000 email credits. You can also opt for a pay-as-you-go plan (if you're not sure how many emails you'll be sending) with SendGrid Lite.

25. Activetrail – activetrail is a full-featured email marketing platform that's totally free for up to 500 subscribers and 2,000 emails per month—perfect if you're a newbie to email marketing and don't yet have a large subscriber list. Paid plans start at $16, and you'll benefit from nearly 100% deliverability, advanced reporting

and management features and much more.

Dedicated Email Marketing Server Software

The dedicated email marketing software is a software that can be downloaded and used manually to manage lists and create your email marketing campaigns. Generally, dedicated server software is more preferable than the online email service providers because they can be used to send far larger volumes of emails to a large mailing list. Numbers of emails that can be sent per campaign can range from 500,000 to sometimes 1,000,000 emails per time, when using a dedicated email marketing server software. A few are listed below:

1. G-lock Easy mail 7: This is a dedicated email marketing software that runs using the Amazon SES (Simple Email Service) platform. The Amazon SES platform is a bulk email sending platform that is cost effective in sending large volumes of emails. Prices for bulk emails on Amazon SES are as low as $1 for 10,000 emails sent.

However, the Amazon SES requires an email sending application on which it would run & that is where the G-lock Easy mail 7 software comes in. To have access to the Amazon SES platform, you must create an account on Amazon's web services website www. aws.amazon.com/ses/. Once your account has been created, head over to G-lock Easy mail 7 website & download the software. It is available as trial software for 14 days, after which you pay $159 for a year. G-lock Easy email 7 is an efficient email marketing software, with functionalities for auto responder emails, and detailed reports of email recipient behaviors.

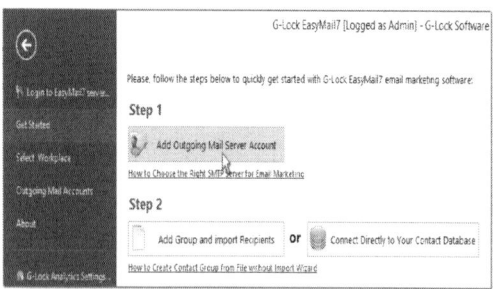

2. Sendy: This is another dedicated email marketing software that also runs on Amazon's SES platform. Sendy is an efficient email marketing software as it has functionalities for auto

responders also known as 'drip campaigns', and accurate reports on every campaign sent with detailed statistics on bounce rates, email open rates, and click through rates. Sendy also is premium software, with a one-time fee of $59.

Sendy

Send newsletters, 100x cheaper
via Amazon SES

Magento integration extension

Now that we have discovered the platforms on which we can create our email marketing campaign based on our preferences and budget, let's move on to tips to creating a high converting email campaign.

CHAPTER SEVEN
TIPS TO CREATING A HIGH CONVERTING EMAIL CAMPAIGN

TIPS TO CREATING A HIGH CONVERTING EMAIL CAMPAIGN

1. Simplicity Rules

I've found that, when people first start considering their email design, they look at the pro designed e-mails that experts in the email marketing industry send out, and think they have to do something equally fancy. But, unless you're competing with a fancy pro email designer, I'll advice you to keep your templates as simple as possible.

Employ the 'KISS' rule: "Keep It So Simple"

2. Plain Text Is Here to Stay

If you're selling software, an information product, or a one-time offer, it's far better to simplify your e-mail process. Things don't get any simpler than plain text. The truth is your e-mails don't have to be fancy. Sending simple, personalized, plain text looking e-mails that almost look like they could have come from a friend goes a long way. The only problem is, most email marketers get this wrong. However, don't let your email look like an essay.

3. Mix It Up

There are two areas where you can mix things up when it comes to your e-mails. The first is personalization. For example, some emails can say "Hi Peter" in the first line? Once upon a time, recipients would have been amazed by this level of personalization in an e-mail, but at this point "Hi {Name}" is often overused. Not that it's not effective anymore, but rather, it's far better to mix up your email with personalization. Start adding personalized snippets elsewhere in the body of your email. For example; "We really want to make sure you're successful, Peter" will still wow people, as will inserting someone's name into the subject line.

The second area you can mix things up is by rotating the type of e-mails you send. Don't just send plain text e-mails alone all the time, send pretty ones also? These pretty e-mails should still be simply designed, but should just be a bit fancier than your plain-text looking emails. Your e-mail template should include a faint line around the content, the company logo, easy to read typography, and blue links or hyperlinks? That's exactly what will catch your potential client's interest.

4. Always Include These Design Elements

There are five design elements you should include in any e-mail template to give it a professional look.

- **Put a light box around the content,** ideally on a white background. Remember, the whole point is to make your e-mails as easy to read as possible. A fine line helps tell the reader's eye where to stop when reading.

- **Include your logo.** It's very important that the reader knows who this email is coming from, and also starts associating your logo with trustworthiness, good content, integrity, and fun insights.

- **Make your typography easy to read.** Your email font (Serif or Sans Serif) doesn't matter as much as the size of the font, and spacing between lines. 14px font size is ideal to create your email.

- **Incorporate text links or hyperlinks.** Make sure your email has 2-3 places where the text acts as a hyperlink. What's more, it's important your text links appear in dark blue, following the norm across the internet. Don't get inventive here with crazy colors that have no meaning.

- **Always include a button.** In addition to text links, a button hyperlink is very important for catching the attention of the eye.

An example of this kind of email is shown below:

5. Mobile Responsiveness Is Required

Mobile responsiveness used to be cutting edge, and very much optional. But, with 65% of all emails nowadays being opened first on a mobile device, mobile responsiveness of your email is a must. This brings us once again to an earlier stressed point, the value of plain text emails, as they will always show up well on a mobile device. Trust me, you don't want to send out emails that most mobile users cannot read, so the issue of mobile responsiveness cannot be overemphasized.

6. Keep Your Fancy E-Mails Simple and Experiment with Animation

Sometimes it can be fun to add a little more design-time and complexity to your e-mails. A nice picture or graphics can make a huge difference on your email's appearance. For sure, this takes longer, but if you're doing a major product release or announcement, it can make a lot of sense. The important thing is to make sure that you keep your fancy e-mails simple and professional.

7. Test Everything

When designing new e-mail templates, it's essential that you test them for compatibility in different e-mail clients. New e-mail templates break all the time, and there are a couple things you can do to minimize this risk.

Keep things simple. The approach I've been advocating here should do wonders across different clients with full compatibility. However you must always put yourself in the receiving end of your emails, and see how they will apply to your recipients.

Use a service like Litmus to test across devices and clients. Litmus allows you to upload an e-mail and preview it in everything from Outlook to Gmail. It's, quite frankly, an essential service if you don't want your e-mails to break and scatter into a mess of code when your potential customers open them.

**These tips are essential to give your email a professional look, and I would recommend you implement most of them.
Please take note of this very important tip:**

"ALWAYS USE A PROFESSIONAL AND CATCHY SUBJECT FOR YOUR EMAILS TO IMPROVE OPEN RATES & REDUCE SPAM ALERTS"

e.g. "Make $2,500 now!" looks like a catchy subject for your email but this subject will most definitely land your email in the spam folder of your recipients' emails. On the other hand, a subject like, "A special secret, just for you", will have a high open rate, and will considerably end up in the inbox of most of your recipients emails.

CHAPTER EIGHT
FINAL WORDS ON EMAIL MARKETING

Now that we've gone through a lot on email marketing, I employ you to begin building your mailing list if you haven't done so. To help you jumpstart your business with email marketing, I am offering anyone who is interested, my comprehensive database of nationwide emails which can serve as your mailing list. Click on this link to access this wonderful package I'm offering for a limited time.

Now, my fellow email marketer, with all you know, I employ you to put it to work with your business to see tremendous growth and conversions for your business. The profits of email marketing may not show instantly, but with consistency and a desire to see your business succeed online, I can assure you that email marketing will take your business to a whole new level. A pro in internet marketing once said, "The money is in the list". I've also come to discover from years of experience that the money is also in the authority of the list builder. Start mailing profitable products to your list, & very soon you'll be a trusted name & brand in the hearts and minds of your list members. With proper email marketing, your limits are beyond the sky!
See your business at the top!

Made in the USA
Middletown, DE
07 January 2026